CRAIG TRADING

CRAIG HAUGAARD MADE 300.9% IN HIS WORLD CUP TRADING CHAMPIONSHIPS® ACCOUNT IN 2014

WANT TO KNOW HOW?

BY LARRY JACOBS

ISBN-13: 978-1511944106

ISBN-10: 1511944102

Trading futures involves significant risk of loss and is not suitable for everyone. Past performance is not necessarily indicative of future results.

TABLE OF CONTENTS

NOTE TO READERS

Please remember that futures trading involves significant risk of loss and is not suitable for everyone, and that past performance is not necessarily indicative of future results. World Cup Championships (WCC) accounts do not necessarily represent all the trading accounts controlled by a given competitor. WCC competitors may control accounts that produce results substantially different than the results achieved in their WCC accounts. WCC entrants may trade more than one account in the competition. For official WCC rules and information, visit the championship web site. Craig Haugaard's AgTrader account in the WorldCupAdvisor.com leader-follower AutoTrade program was entered in the 2014 World Cup Championship of Futures Trading and has continued to trade after the conclusion of the competition. Accounts trading in the WCC may be subject to commission rates different from those following the AutoTrade program. AgTrader's net return in the World Cup Championship is higher than the program's net return in the WCA AutoTrade program due to commission differential and the absence of subscription fees in contest calculations. At the end of the competition through Dec. 31, 2014, the WCA AutoTrade net return was 255.8% compared to Craig's 300.9% return in the contest. As of March 31, 2015, the greatest cumulative percentage decline (drawdown) in month-end net equity during the life of the AgTrader AutoTrade program on WorldCupAdvisor.com is -28.8% (2/28/14 to 6/30/14).

An investor must read, understand and sign a Letter of Direction for WorldCupAdvisor.com leader-follower programs before investing. This e-book contains statements of opinion.

INTRODUCTION

I want to thank you and congratulate you for downloading this book. This book contains an interview in Chapter 1 with Craig Haugaard, third-place FINISHER IN THE 2014 WORLD CUP Championship of Futures Trading® with a 300.9% net profit.

In the rest of the book I will explain to you the indicators that he said he used in the interview. You can then actually see and understand how they work. I am not going to tell you exactly how Craig Huagaard used the tools to make his 300.9% return on a $10,000 investment. That information is not public and belongs only to Craig Huagaard. He spent 15 years developing his trading techniques. Here are the indicators that he said he used:

>Seasonality
>MACD
>Stochastics
>Moving Averages
>Trailing Stops
>Fibonacci Retracements & Extensions

All of the charts in this book are produced using my favorite charting software Market-Analyst®. I have also arranged for you to get a trial so that you might have the chance to actually work with these indicators with a live charting platform; See Chapter 13 on how to access your FREE trial.

You will also be able to download 6 video presentations that I personally created so you can see how these indicators can be setup and followed in a step-by-step manner. You can access them here:

http://www.worldcupadvisor.com/craigtrading.html

After you understand how these indicators work, I would then recommend that you go to WorldCupAdvisor.com and consider following Craig Haugaard's trades. You can request more information here.

https://www.worldcupadvisor.com/InfoRequest2.aspx?id=1807&t=Y

You will be able to automatically mirror his trades in your own brokerage account with World Cup Leader-Follower AutoTrade™ service. You will also be able to see what his trade looks like on your own charts and better understand why he made the trades. There are no long-term commitments. You can go month-by-month.

For more information about World Cup Advisor, go to Chapter 12.

Next go to Chapter 1 to read the interview with Craig Haugaard.

CHAPTER 1- INTERVIEW WITH CRAIG HAUGAARD

In 2014 Craig Haugaard had a net increase of 300.9% in his trading account in the World Cup Championship of Futures Trading.

The following is an interview with Craig Haugaard regarding how he made his excellent trading return.

As you read this interview, please remember that substantial gains cannot be made without taking substantial risk of loss. Futures trading should only be undertaken with risk capital – that is, capital you can afford to lose. Always consider whether trading is appropriate for you in light of your experience, objectives, financial resources and risk tolerance.

Larry: I understand that you had an increase of 300.9% in last year's World Cup Trading Championship. How did you do that?

Craig: I work with producers trying to get them to make sales in the market when they ought to be making sales. Many times these producers get hung up in fundamentals. They always tend to wait longer and not get the best prices. I have put together something that I though made sense using historical seasonal yearly tendencies. I use it along with some technical indicators to help them hedge their crops. This is a system to help producers make their sales at better prices. On paper it looks great. The producers that bought into it so far are having some success. I do get a lot of questions. Many of the producers ask me what is my track record so I decided to enter this contest to establish a "tested in live fire" track record. This is something I worked on for the last 15 years.

It was sort of a marketing philosophy that I have come up with that seems to make sense.

Larry: What was your background before you started this?

Craig: I have been with this company for about 3 years and before that another 8 years with a large COOP. I came on their hedge desk then was asked to start their grain origination program for them. Before that I was with the extension service for about 10 years. With them I was a specialist in risk management. I did a lot of seminars about risk management. I wrote some articles for Top Producer Magazine. I was asked to speak at a few national events such as The Commodity Classic.

Larry: How did you decide to compete in the World Cup Championship?

Craig: I had been aware of it since the 1980s. I watched Larry Williams make a big splash. So I knew it was out there and I wanted a live platform to try out my ideas. This would be the premier place to do it. I would get more attention than with any other platform. It seems just to be the natural way to go and gravitate toward this contest.

Larry: Again how did you get your outstanding performance of 300.9% return in the contest last year?

Craig: There are some years that give you some opportunities and last year was one of them. I was in a market that gave me an outstanding gain. There was a big decrease in prices. I was short corn and beans and probably more in beans than anything. There was a significant downturn. The system I put together that I used for farmers to hedge worked perfectly in trading in this contest. I made some good sales for producers very early in the season. My first sales in Soybeans were around $12.40 and eventually traded down to the low $9.00 area. It did not take a lot of brilliance to ride that horse. I left more money on the table than I should have because I did not have the right discipline that I should have at the end. It kind of got away from me. It was an excellent year with great opportunity. I was fortunate to have taken advantage of some of it.

Larry: What did you use for your ideas in your trading? Did you use indicators, fundamentals or what?

Craig: If you look at corn and beans there is a seasonal trend. Just look at the price of December Corn for example on June 15th to October 15th and you will see that roughly 75% of the time the price is lower on October 15th than it was on June 15th. It's about the same percentage for soybeans but maybe a little later starting at July 10th. I started with the base idea that there is a seasonal pattern there. Prices usually go down. Some years this is not the case for example with a drought. But with most years this is a normal situation.

Once I have identified the seasonal time periods that I want to make sales in I then turn to technicals to fine-tune when to make those sales. I use a combination of three indicators to fine-tune when seasonal trades should be made. Not using anything fancy just moving averages, stochastics and MACD. If I get all three of those telling me the same story at a time I know we should be making sales, I have a lot of confidence of putting those trades on.

Larry: Do you have any special settings for those?

Craig: I have tweaked them around a little bit but I ended up just using the standard settings. Whoever set the standard settings did a pretty good job with it.

Larry: What about cycles? For example some people use a 45-week high or a 20-week high/low etc. Did you use anything like that?

Craig: My dad traded quite a bit, used Elliott Wave and all of that. I just have never used them. What I use works pretty well. I think there are certain times when I would rather be long or short using seasonal tendencies. I don't use any wave or cycle theories. Those that use them may be dead on right, but I have not picked up on it. I'll use some calendar dates that I'll want to be in a short position or a long position. I don't know if it is right or wrong, I am just trying to play the odds in my favor as much as I can.

Larry: What do you do about grain reports? Do you get out or stay in?

Craig: Last year I stayed in through them. We have one coming up tomorrow. I started up lightening up today. I don't think it a very big report, but right now at this time of the year there are a lot of uncertainties. There are a lot of things we don't know now about plantings. I don't know about weather yet either. Until we know more it is going to be a volatile market. I am little more cautious right now. I am now more on the sidelines than I normally would be. In other parts of the year I might stay in more in the market.

Larry: What about stops? Do you use them?

Craig: I used them quite a bit last year. I had to adjust them daily. I keep them tight so positions don' get away from me. I use stops a lot more now to make sure I don't let winners turn into losers.

Larry: Do you trade a lot?

Craig: I hold positions a lot more than most folks. Last year I had 88 trades. I did not realize that I traded that much. This year I think I am around 12 to 15 trades. I am not in a great deal. I feel a little better with the positions I have now. My job would not really allow me to be in and out a lot. I could not justify a lot of trading.

Larry: Do you put all your positions on at once and ride them all the way up to the top and get out?

Craig: I put on a little at a time and then add to the positions. Then I will get out gradually, not all at once. I take a little off the table as the market goes into where the prices I think are going. Last year I started out short in Soybeans and as the prices dropped I was using some Fibonacci projections trying to find out where support levels were. When we broke through support I added to short positions.

Larry: How does this work with World Cup Advisor and people following your trades?

Craig: This is a learning experience with me.

Larry: Do they just follow your trades or are the automatically put in?

Craig: When I make a trade it kicks them in. I can't have a price target so I have to use a market order, because they are guaranteeing that we all get in or out at the same price. It changed a little the way I trade. It didn't have a big impact on me. Not that I don't put thought into my trades, but I may be a little more deliberate in my trading since other people's money is depending on my trades. If I am an idiot and I lose my own money that's one thing, but losing other people's money is another thing. Other people trust me to conduct due diligence and come out with well-thought-out trades. I have done stupid trades in the past that I should never have done. I am just a couple months into it now. So far folks are making money and liking it. It's been an interesting experience.

Larry: I know several big traders who trade fantastically, with their own money, but when they try to trade other people's money they can't do it. So it's excellent that it is working out with you.

Craig: Last year when I first showed up on the leader board it was a goofy feeling and I ended up doing trades that I should not have done. It was a psychological struggle for me for a little while. When I got through it I was able to go back and evaluate myself and analyze my actions. The human mind is sometimes crazy. You need to get it corralled or you will end up doing irrational things. I got through that battle and it was interesting. I learned a lot about myself there. I went through some soul searching.

Larry: What about Commitment of Traders Report? Do you use that?

Craig: I look at it but I don't make decisions based on what is reported, but I am aware of it and I watch it.

Larry: What about fundamentals?

Craig: I just get besieged by them daily. It's my job. I trade about 80 million bushels of cash grain a year. I am always in that market dealing with export terminals or whatever. Farmers want to talk fundamentals. If it sprinkles in Brazil I am aware of it. Yes, I am immersed in it. Does it impact my trading? I think to an extent. I try to keep the emotion out of it as much as I can. I try to let the technical indicators help me as much as they can with timing. If you look at the grain market 25% of the time the market will rally between June and October. It is based on fundamental changes. So I need to be aware of any fundamental change. If something is going to change fundamentally I want to be out in front of it as fast as possible. One needs to marry fundaments with technical factors in the market.

Larry: What about weather?

Craig: My big problem with weather is like everyone else's problem, you tend to look at your back yard. I struggled with that a couple years ago, we had a drought in our trade area but the rest of the nation was doing great. I had to keep it to myself. It had a big effect on our producers. You need to remind yourself that what you see outside of your window is not the world. It's easy to get emotionally involved with the weather. I see farmers making bad decisions all the time based on their own weather.

Larry: When you wake up in the morning and come into the office what do you look at?

Craig: I look at the charts and look to see what is happening overnight. I also look at 20 different fundamental reports and try to skim through and highlight anything important as fast as possible. Then we are off to the races.

Larry: What services do you like to work with and what time frame charts - daily, weekly, intra-day?

Craig: I use DTN and that's what I have always used since my first COOP job. This is the package I look at. I'm sure there are others out there that are just as good or even better. It's a comfort area with me. It allows me to do what I do. I look at the daily, weekly and monthly charts. I look at weekly charts a lot. When I am putting on or taking off a trade I will look at 30- and 60-minute charts so I can fine-tune my entries.

Larry: Do you believe in day-trading?

Craig: It doesn't work for me. I know it works for some others. I could never do it, especially with my job. I don't think I have the temperament for it. It would not be my game. I am pretty sure I would get whipsawed in that game.

Larry: Craig, thank you for the interview and good luck on your trading at World Cup Advisor.

CHAPTER 2- SEASONALITY

Seasonality is the study of average price movements during turning points in the span of a year.

This study essentially originated in agricultural commodity markets. The amount of grain that arrives at harvest time ordinarily drives prices down. Then the product is consumed throughout the rest of the year with increased demand prices typically rise.

This chapter will discuss the ideas behind this study of seasonality and the tool to monitor seasonal patterns.

Cycle analysis has always been a part of technical analysis and seasonality has been a part of it particularly in regard to commodities and the grain market. Supply and demand occurs with imbalances that happen during a year. The harvest pressure of grain coming to market normally drives grain prices down. It is very easy to see how seasonal influences play a major influence in prices especially in grains.

Markets are a discounting type of a mechanism and for that reason it will anticipate the seasonal changes in both supply and demand. That means that tops and bottoms in the market may occur earlier and may jump ahead of the harvest time.

Seasonal timing is not fixed and will not occur the same time each year. There are other factors such as global trade, distribution and supply and demand that also affect prices. For example, the crop production of South America and consumption worldwide can change a normal seasonality tendency.

Soybean prices usually present us with typical price cycles. The Seasonal tops do tend to occur around February, March and April and lows occur July, August and September. The beginning of the drop starts in June as you can see in the following monthly seasonality chart. In this book all charts are made with the software Market-Analyst which I feel does analysis of the markets better than most any other software.

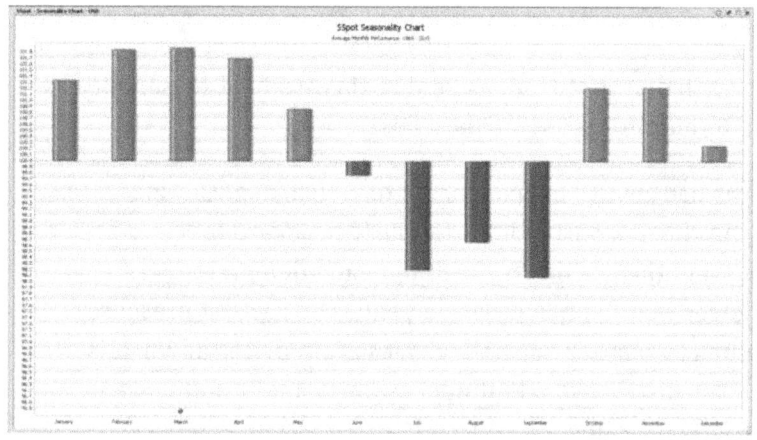

In this next chart see a daily seasonality chart. You will notice that there is a tendency of the market to turn down late June. Notice June 28th is the seasonal beginning of weakness. This weakness was foretold many months ahead of the actual fact.

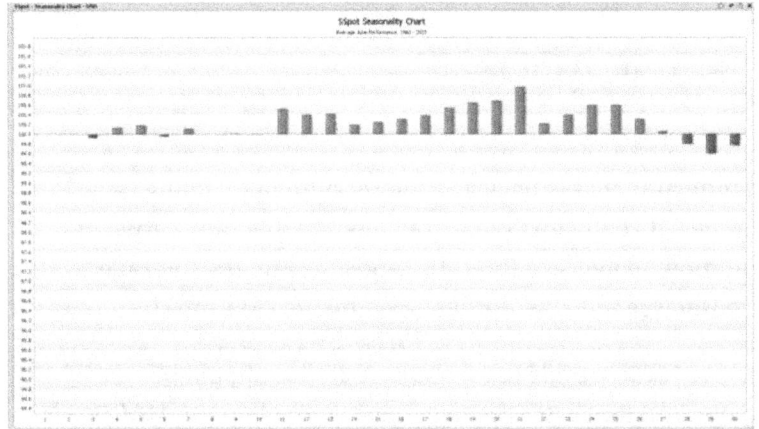

Notice on the actual price chart where the peak of the soybean's price was June 28th. This was the predicted top on the daily seasonality chart. The market turned down after that point and there was a severe drop in prices.

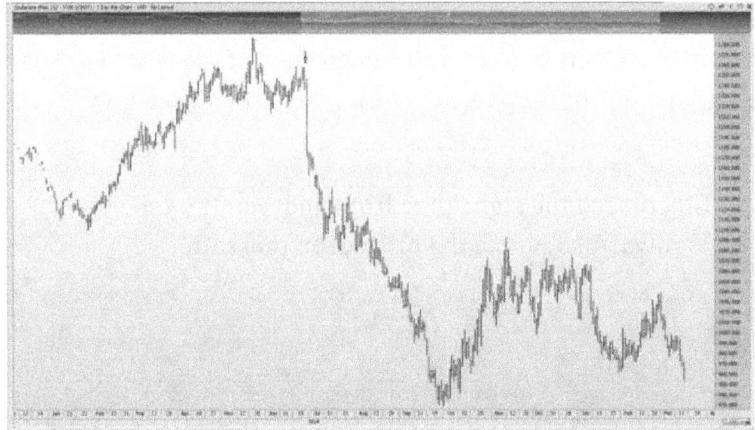

CHAPTER 3- MACD

MACD is an indicator that is basically the refinement of using two moving averages. It really just measures the real distance between two different moving average lines. It stands for Moving Average Convergence Divergence. It was developed by Gerald Appel.

MACD is used to trade trends in the market. It also should be avoided in powerful markets. The signal is taken when the MACD line crosses its signal line which is a 9-day exponential moving average of MACD.

Before you use it make sure the price in a market is trending. If the market is surging then the signal is not reliable.

You should go long a market when the MACD crosses the signal line from below. On the other hand you can go short if the MACD crosses the signal line from above. See the next chart and see how this worked.

Notice the MACD crossed the signal line from above at the time of the two down arrows. Also notice the price drop thereafter.

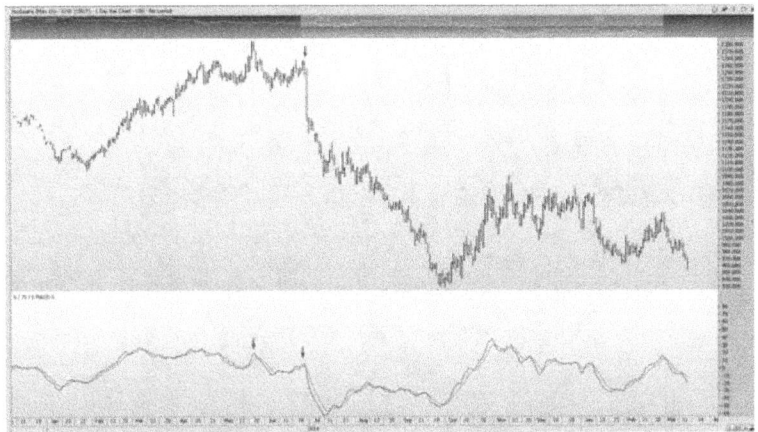

If there is a divergence on the MACD the signal is much stronger.

In the following chart on the first sell arrow the price came back to the top but the MACD did not rise back to the top indicating the market was weak. The market had lost its momentum.

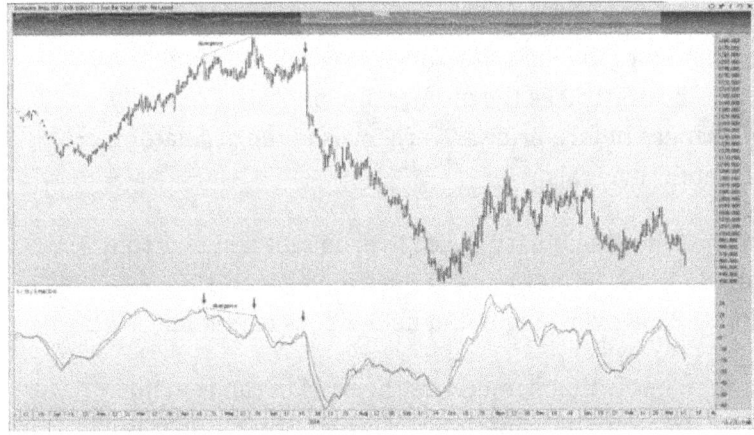

CHAPTER 4- STOCHASTICS

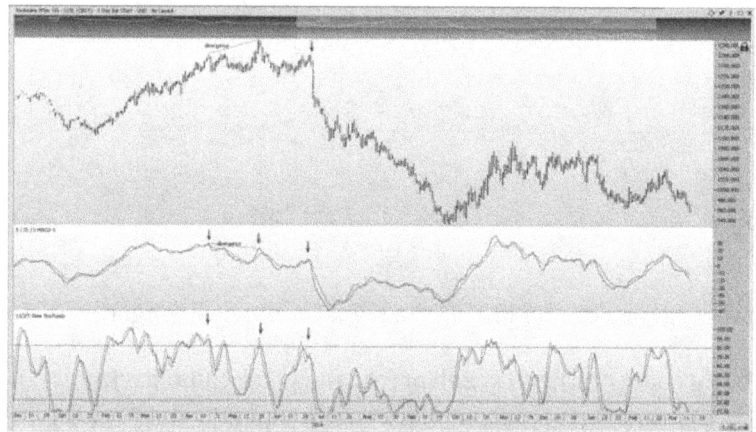

The stochastic oscillator was developed by George Lane in the 1950s. This is a momentum oscillator that displays the position of the close in relation to the high-low range over a fixed number of periods. This indicator tracks the momentum of price. Generally momentum changes before price. Divergences in the oscillator can be used to foretell reversals.

This oscillator does make it easy to see overbought and oversold areas. The oscillator is setup to in a range from zero to 100. Normally above 80 is overbought and below 20 is oversold.

It is important to know that sometimes the market can remain overbought or oversold for sometimes in strong trends. So this oscillator may not work well during those time periods.

Normally a move above 80 and then a downturn below it is bearish signal while a move below 20 and a turn back up is considered a bullish signal.

Divergences happen when a new high or new low is not confirmed by the oscillator. Bullish divergence happens when price records a lower low but the oscillator forms a higher low. That shows lost momentum. A bearish divergence forms when prices record a higher high but the oscillator forms a lower high showing lost momentum.

Another reliable stochastic oscillator signal is to have divergence in the oscillator and then have the price break support and at the same time cross the 50 line. That is usually a major turn signal.

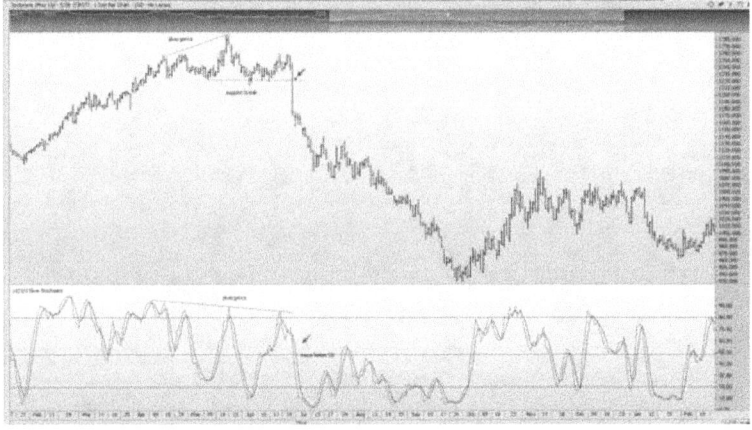

Another signal that you should know about is if the oscillator makes a higher high than the previous peak then you can buy the next bottom and conversely if the market makes a lower low than the previous low then you can sell the next high.

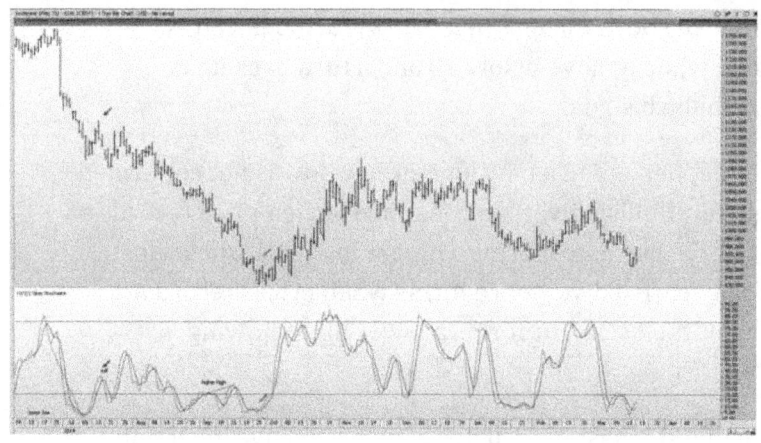

Chapter 5 – Moving Averages

Now how to use moving averages. The first step is to find the average that best fits the market. Then double it, double it again and then half it.

In the following chart I used Market-Analyst to determine the best moving average that fit the chart. It happened to be the 20-moving average. How to find the best moving average is discussed in the video presentations.

20MA

Now find the other important averages. I calculated them as follows:

2 x 20MA = 40MA
4 x 20MA = 80MA
20MA / 2 = 10MA

The following chart has only the 20MA on it. You get a signal when prices move above the average and close there for two days. Then you can buy the market. When prices move under the moving average and close there for two days sell the market.

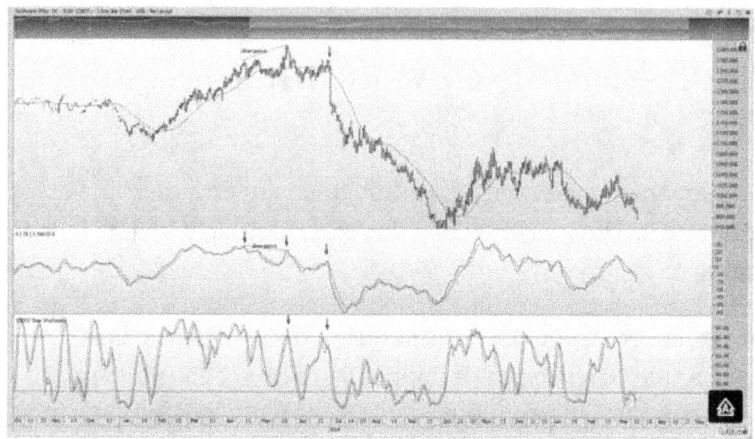

The following chart has all 4 averages on it. When the average cross each other the market changes direction.

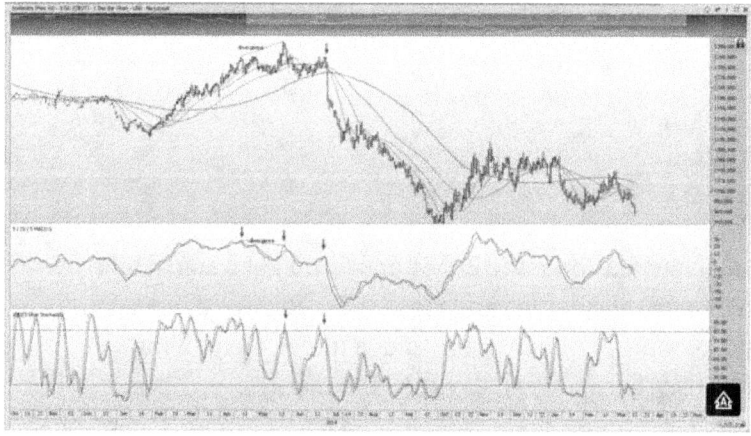

Moving averages are more of a confirmation of the other indicators. They are a lagging signal. You will find that the MACD and Stochastics give you an earlier signal than moving aveages.

CHAPTER 6 – TRAILING STOPS

Using trailing stops many experts agree is a necessity. They limit losses and protect gains. But there are two problems using trailing stops.

1) One problem is that a sudden movement in a market due to a temporary market reaction to some possible news might just trigger an unwanted sell stop loss.

2) Another problem might be a big price gap down on the open between the close of the market of the prior day and the opening of the next day. This is usually due to some negative news. There is little that you can do about that.

Many traders use the simple moving average and apply that to a daily stop and they will put their stop a certain percentage below it from 1% up to 10%.

Another stop system many use is the Chandelier stop. It was introduced by Alexander Elder in his 2002 book Come into My Trading Room. It uses a multiple of the average true range from highs during an uptrend and then it adds them to lows during any down trend. See the following chart using the Chandelier stop on Soybeans.

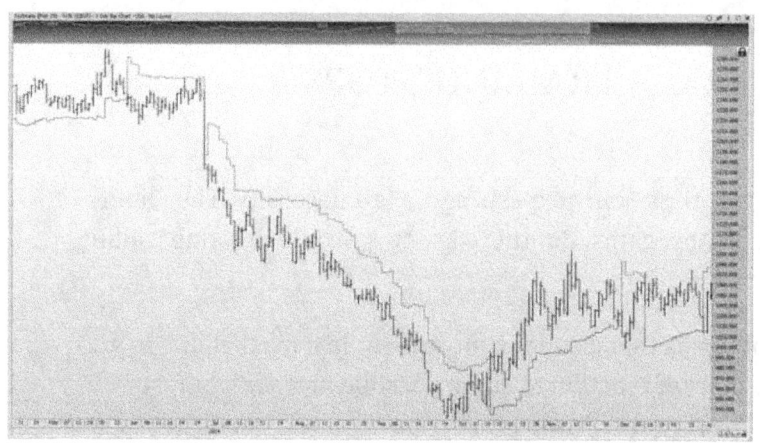

28

CHAPTER 7 – FIBONACCI RETRACEMENT & EXTENSIONS

Leonardo de Pisa de Fibonacci was born in Italy, and was educated in North Africa. Leonardo was taught mathematics in Bugia and often travelled with his father who was a diplomat. He put a lot of thought into mathematics and figured out Fibonacci numbers that occur in nature almost everywhere.

His discoveries were amazing and proved that the market was in fact orderly and not a disordered place as most people thought it was.

The Commodity market represents interactions between individuals. The ebb and flow of the market can be explained by Fibonacci where humans interact.

The Fibonacci Numerical Sequence

The Fibonacci sequence was discovered by Fibonacci and the sequence is as follows: The sum of the previous two numbers will always equal the next number in the sequence. See below:

1+1=2 13+21=34

1+2=3 21+34=55

2+3=5 34+55=89

3+5=8 55+89=144

5+8=13 89+144=233

8+13=21 144+233=377 and to infinity

This sequence is relevant to the commodity markets. By using this sequence of numbers you can get price levels and trade them to your advantage.

The market waves move in a Fibonacci sequence and can become very predictable when you know how to use the Fibonacci tool for both retracements and extensions.

Fibonacci Retracement Lines

The true way to find Fibonacci retracements is to first start at the low of the move and then stop at the exact top of the trend. The charting software will then calculate retracement price levels such as:

38.3%

50%

61.8%

See the following charts. When the prices dropped under the levels the market became weak.

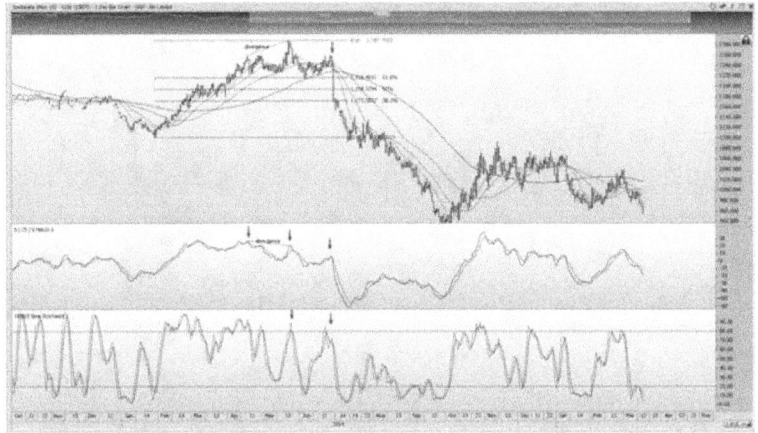

Fibonacci extensions can be used to tell where the market is headed. In the next chart the .61.8%, the 100% and the 161.8% projections were made.

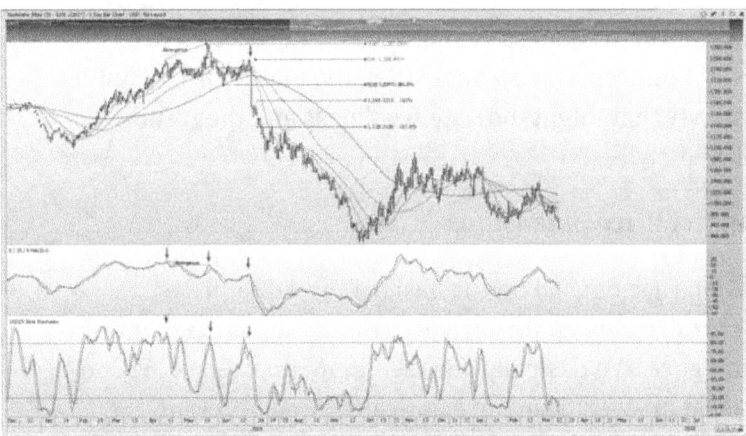

In the next chart you can see the new projection levels of 61.8%, and the 100% levels were projected using the Fibonacci extention tool.

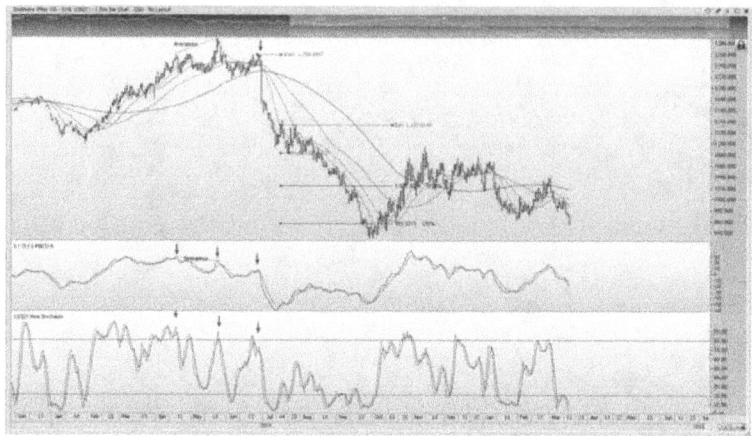

The rule is that the longer the time frame of the move is the more relevant are the Fibonacci levels. When the market is in a strong uptrend and starts to pull back, it is considered quite healthy to have a pull back to the 38.2% and even the 50% level. Any more might be considered weakness. Sometimes it can react up to the 61.8% and if it bounces back strongly then the market is OK, but if it bounces slowly that might indicate weakness and the trend might break shortly.

Using Fibonacci Price Extensions

Price Extensions are figured on the basis of the 1-2-3 price movement that markets go through. It is the 2nd move up that we are trying to figure. We basically use the Fibonacci ratio of .618 to give us the right answer. There are basically three different numbers that give us the right projections. They are:

.618

1.00

1.618

To find out the first target take the price movement x and just multiply it by .618 and then you just measure it from the retracement. The second target is exactly the same as x and the third target just multiple the x by 1.618.

The charting software does this all for you to calculate the Fibonacci Levels. The first thing to do is just drag the Fibonacci Tool from the high of the move down to the low then click the mouse then move it up to the high of the retracement and click the mouse. It then calculates the projections.

Using Both Fibonacci Retracements and Extensions

You can also use both price retracements and price extensions at the same time. This will be explained in the video presentations using Fibonacci.

CHAPTER 8 – USING DIFFERENT TIME FRAMES

The Daily Time Frame is where you spend almost all of your time as a trader. This is where most of the opportunities will occur. Your daily charts to be effective really need to go back as far as 7 months or more. This will give you then enough data so that can formulate your technical tools such as the MACD, Stochastics and Moving Averages. You'll also have enough data and swings so you can calculate the Fibonacci swings and extensions.

The Weekly Time Frame allows you to really just step back and get a bigger look at the long term trend. You know you can only fit so many daily bars on your chart depending on the size of your screen. With a weekly chart you can go back much further. You can also see the major trends plus major support and resistance levels. Also you will be able to do larger Fibonacci retracements and extensions.

The 30 and 60 Minute Chart is really like you are getting a microscope and analyzing what is going on with the charts on a micro scale level. All of the same principals can be applied to the smaller charts as you did with the daily charts. Fibonacci retracements and extensions work nicely on these charts.

The 5 Minute Chart is even a more micro level than the 30 and 60 minute chart. You are really zoomed in with this level. For many this may be too close. All the same principals still work that worked on the larger daily charts.

Tips to Use the Different Time Frames

It's important to know that each time frame does affect the other. If some news report, in grains for example a grain report, it will affect the 5 minute chart and that affects the 30 and 60 minute chart. That affects the daily chart. And that affects the weekly chart.

By using a smaller time frame you might be able to get a tighter stop loss rather than using the daily chart.

Using different multiple time frames can really give you a better feel of the market and will improve your trading success. You will never find a perfect chart on the weekly, daily or smaller intraday charts. You main goal is to spot the main trend of the market using all of the different time frames at your disposal.

Always pick your time frame and then look at the time frame just above it. So if you are using a daily chart then look at the weekly time frame. You can also look at the time frame just below it such as a 60 minute chart.

Next is a daily soybean chart using the 20 day moving average.

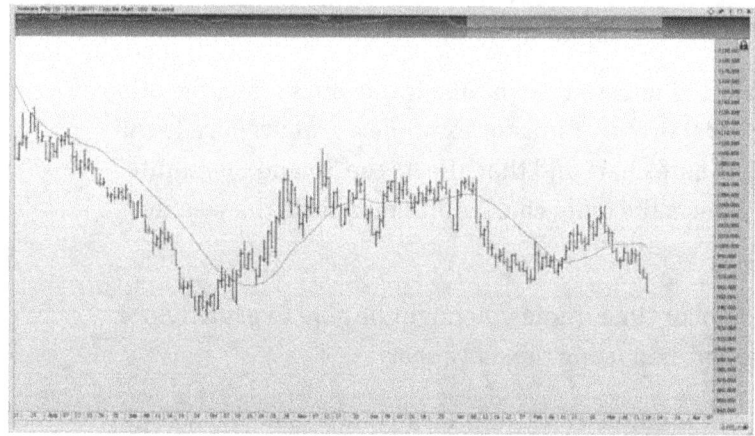

Now look at the weekly chart using a 20 week moving averge. See the difference.

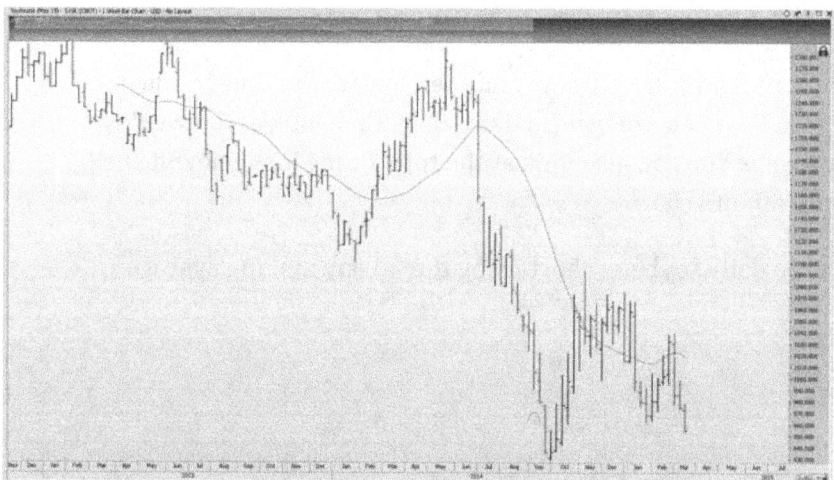

You can put on the chart what is called a higher time frame moving average. This is a 10 bar weekly moving average placed over the daily chart. So you will know when both the daily and the weekly chart changes direction. This chart take the place of both a daily and a weekly chart.

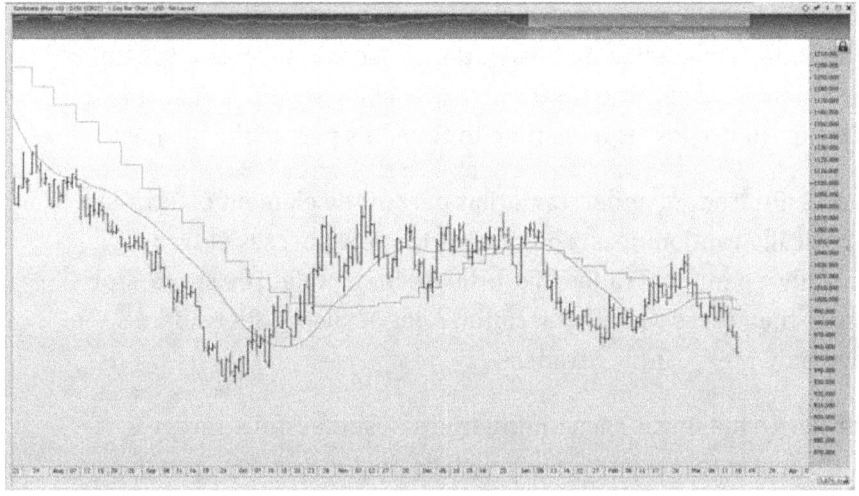

Chapter 9 – Money Management

Why some traders win and why others lose has a whole lot to do with money management rather than picking winners. All traders will experience losses from time to time. It's part of the business.

Successful traders understand that part of the element of a trade is basically randomness. That means that the success of trading is partially a gamble. Trades that lose are inevitable. The successful trader then takes that into account. A lot of successful traders have only 50% winning trades!

The key to making 50% winning trades a successful strategy is to let the winners make twice as much as the loosers do. Then that profit can take care of the losers plus give you an overall profit.

Why do losers lose in the markets? It's simple, they really don't allow for a bunch of losing trades in a row. It will happen to most traders sooner or later.

So the difference is that successful traders structure there trades so that they produce a two-to-one profit/loss ratio. That allows the trader to succeed over the long term.

Also we spend a large amount of time trying to figure out the best time to get in and when to get out of trades. But just as important is how we get in and out. A trader needs to look at scaling in and the scaling out of positions.

Why should a trader scale into a position over time? The reason is to enhance their gain. A trader should start off a trade with a small position and then only add to it when it is winning. Then he only risks a little to make a lot.

Scaling out of a trade is also recommended. Instead of letting a trade hit a profit target and closing out the whole position, instead only close out a part of the position and let the balance of the trade have an opportunity to move much further into more profit. This actually secures part of the profit and lets the door open for even more gains.

Many traders will move their stop to break even as soon as an initial target is hit leaving the ability to have much more profit.

Now that you understand the benefit of scaling, you should only add to positions that are profitable and not add to losing positions. Don't throw good money to the bad if the trade is proving you wrong. You have heard of cutting losers short.

There is also no reason to scale out of a losing trade. Just get out of it if it is proving you wrong.

It is also wise to set 2 or 3 profit targets for a trade instead of just 1.

You must understand that trading with logic in how we enter and exit your trades is important. It can enhance your profit and reduce your risk.

CHAPTER 10- PUTTING IT ALL TOGETHER

So now let's put everything we have learned together.

Here is the step-by-step procedure: (In this case we are looking at the 2014 May Soybeans)

1) First thing look at the monthly seasonality charts. Notice that June is the first month of the year that the market turns weak. It then looks like the market stays weak for up to 4 months. This then seems like an excellent opportunity to short the market. The weather is normal and no droughts.

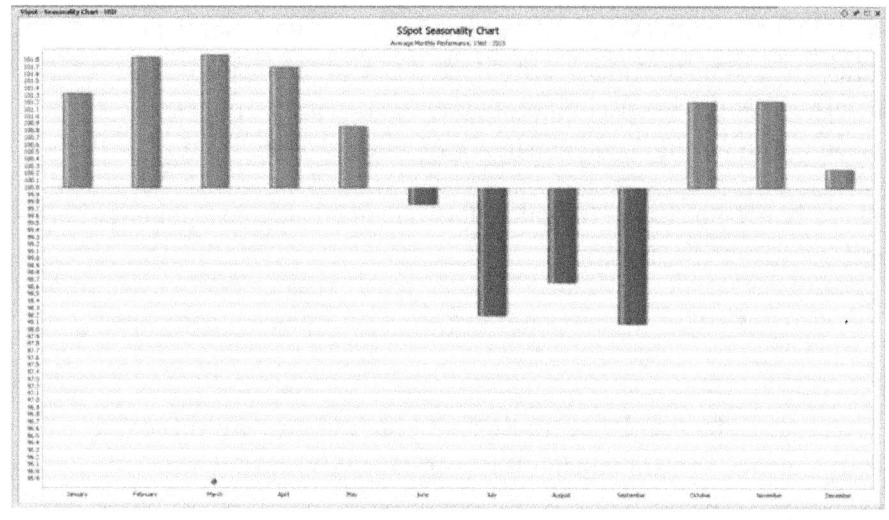

2) So next lets fine tune it and go to the daily seasonality chart. Looking that the daily seasonality chart for June the market turns

weak June 27th – 28th. That is our target area to go short if everything looks good on the charts.

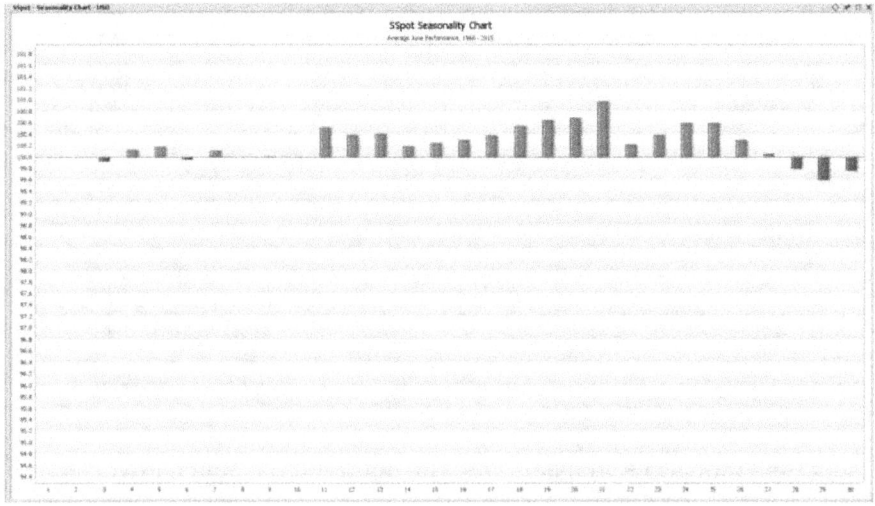

3) Now lets pull up the daily May 2014 Soybean chart. Lets put on the 4 moving averages, stochastics, and MACD. Look at that on June 27th the signals are all there.

a) MACD crossed over from top to bottom giving a short signal. Also there is divergence.

b) Stochastics crossed over from top to bottom giving us a short signal. Also there is divergence.

c) Price have dropped under the 10, 20, 40 and 80 day moving average giving us a short signal.

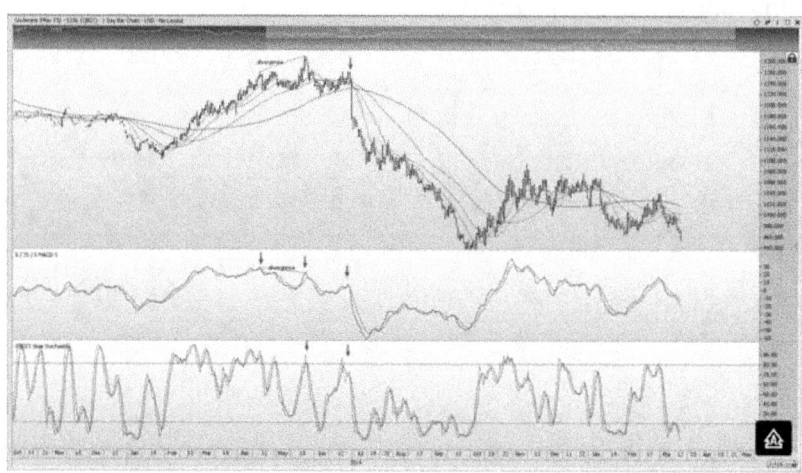

Using the Fibonacci Extension Tool the market looks much lower.

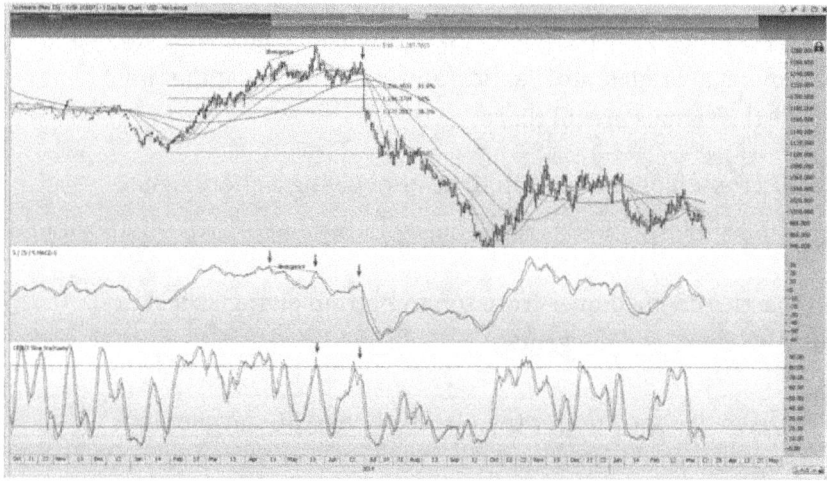

So short the market with your first position at the first arrow and put a protective Chandelier stop above the market and follow the market down. Then short another position at the 2nd arrow. Also protect this position with a Chandelier stop. Then add another short positon at the 3rd arrow. Protect this position with another Chandelier stop.

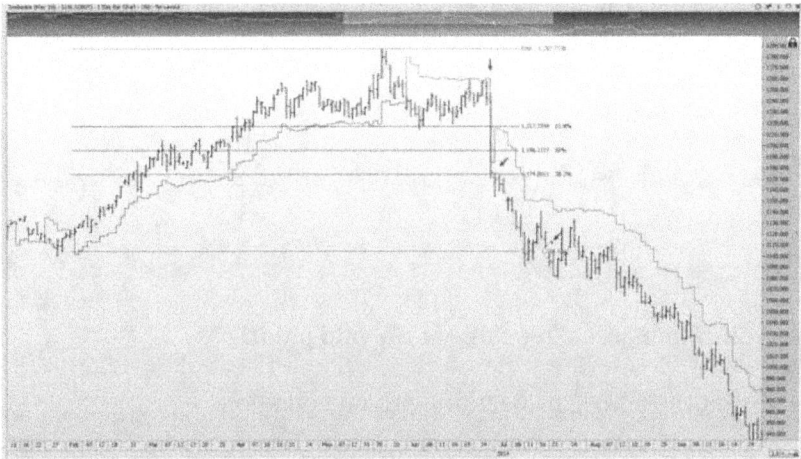

Midway there was another Fibonacci extension projection to about were the market bottomed in October. See chart.

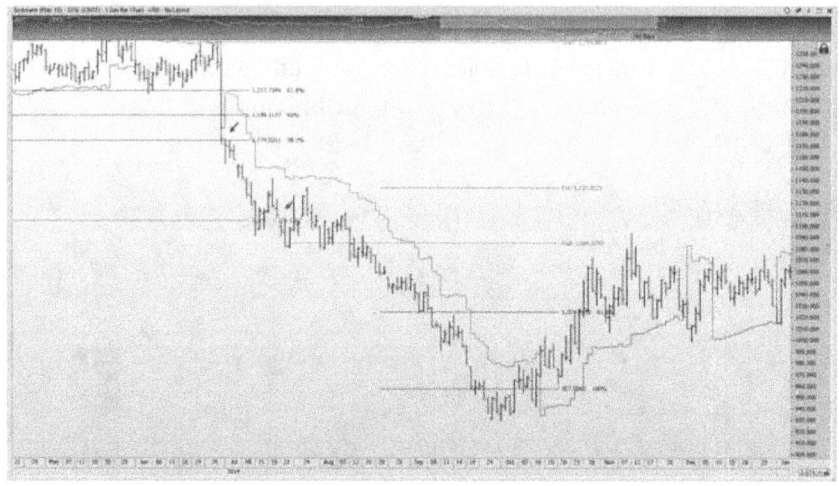

Refigure your Fibonacci extensions at the mid point.

Take profits at the 61.8% projection with one position.

Take profits on the second position at the 100% projection.

Keep a trailing stop on the last position. Stopped out on October 10th with the last position with the Chandelier stop.

Also notice that the daily seasonality chart indicated the market would turn up around October 10th which it did.

Watching the video presentations will make this much clearer.

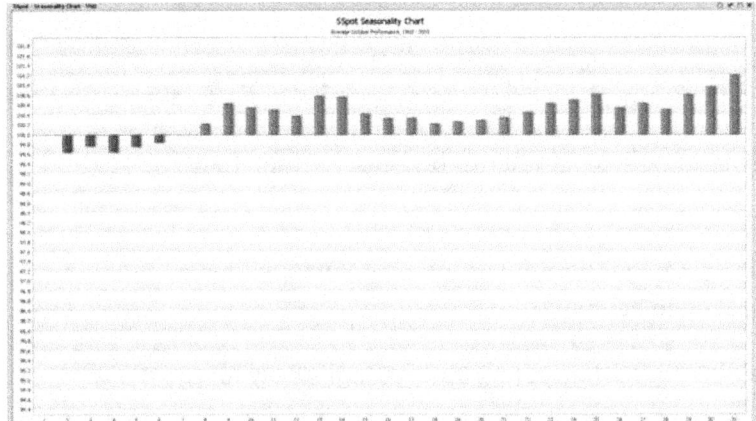

CHAPTER 11 – NEGATIVE THINKING

For most people it is just simpler to be negative than to be positive.

We are in a society that does focus on what you don't have than rather what you do have.

If we then don't have what others have then it's easy for most of us just to call it everyone else's fault.

Many traders blame they losses on other people or a conspiracy against them.

These negative thoughts embed into our psyches cause us to dwell on everything bad in our lives. This hurts are ability to make good decisions for example following the rules of successful trading. What you need to do is to learn to turn off the bad thoughts and switch to the positive thoughts.

I am going to give you some tips and several exercises to help you remove these bad negative thoughts. I can't stress enough to be a successful trader you need to remove all negative thoughts. You need to infuse your mind with constructive positive thoughts and then it will allow you to experience contentment and success in your trading. You will then be inspired to be confident and take action at the right time and achieve success in trading.

Here are some tips and several exercises:

1) Reward yourself when you recognize a negative thought. What I mean is most of us don't recognize when we are being negative. Being negative is second nature for a lot of us. If you can identify when it occurs then you are on the way to correcting your way of thinking. The key to recognize a negative thought and turn it into a positive thing. Reward yourself for that. Identify the negative thought and stop it. Then tell yourself, "good catch"! That replaces the negative thought with a positive one.

2) You need to find what is best in other people. By doing this it will help you to be a positive person. You will not be judging people. That makes you negative. You know that everyone has many flaws, but it is your job to find what is positive in them and then target that positive thing. This will then make you feel much better about even yourself. This will help to make you a positive person and then actually a better trader.

Instead of having a head full of negative thoughts you will have only positive thoughts and that gives you a much better perspective on life and on things around you. You won't be over thinking trading situations and continuing to debate what you should do in a trading situation. You'll do what you are supposed to do. Over analyzing a trade will cause you to just doubt yourself and increase your perspective negatively. This will then prohibit you from making the right trading decisions when you need to make them.

You need to develop a good process of making the right trading decisions. You know the rules of correct trading. Write down the pros and cons of making a correct trade then take the proper action. The key is not being stuck in your uncertainty, inaction and over analysis.

3) Visualize Success. If you are all the time worrying about failing at trading you are setting yourself up for that failure. You need to replace this with a vision of success. See yourself making the right trading decision and making a profitable trade.

4) Develop a process to switch negative thoughts. When you get a negative thought ask yourself, "is this the way I want to feel?" Do you really want these negative thoughts in your life and potentially ruining your trading performance? You will never be happy with negative thoughts in your mind.

Here is an example:

Negative thought: I don't know how to handle what the market is doing right now?

Positive thought: This is my opportunity to learn how to trade this situation and learn something brand new.

When you are faced with a conflict you can comes to terms with it and create a positive outcome.

You need to develop many switches to turn negatives into positives. This will empower yourself. Write down the switches and continue to repeat them daily. In your trading you will get many curve balls that will make things difficult and turning a negative into a positive may seems impossible, but you can do it. Have confidence in yourself. Eventually you will have a more positive attitude over time and will find much more satisfaction in your trading and in your life.

To stay motivated can be a daily concern but you need to think about the benefits you will reap by just incorporating this way of thinking. Positive will do this for you:

a) You will be a positive person

b) You will have more satisfaction in life

c) You will be pleasant to be around

d) You will be content

e) You will believe in successful trading

f) You will build successful trading skills

g) You will have ability to adapt to different trading situations

h) You will reduce your stress and that will help your long term health

i) Your positive behavior will be contagious to others around you and they will be positive to you.

You need to keep in mind that if you have been negative for a long time it won't be easy to turn this around. You may have many years of negative thoughts in your head. But you can program your brain to make it positive and successful in trading. To have positive thinking will take a lot of time and practice. You must change your thoughts if you want to be successful in trading.

You should get a journal and start recording your journey. Write down your positive thoughts and the barriers that you need to break through. You will find it is much easier each and every day to be positive over time. Then after a while all the negative thoughts will disappear leaving your mind with positive thoughts and your will be a more happy person, a successful person and enjoyable to be around.

Another thing that will help you is to surround yourself with positive and successful people. You are really the average of the people that you spend the most time with. So when you start this changing of your negative thoughts it is important that you have supportive and positive people around you.

Psychologists have written many articles on how important it is to surround you with positive people. People need to reinforce your positive attitude. The way to do this is to take stock of 20 people who know and then ask what was their disposition and how did they make you feel when you were around them. Was it supportive for you? Were they positive or negative?

Choose the people that were positive and try to spend more free time with them over the next 90 days. These people will be the key for you to change your negative thoughts. Only you can take the responsibility for changing your life. You need to think positively no matter what the situation is.

I have covered what I see for you to be a more positive and a successful trader. You can unleash the infinite power inside of yourself and be a successful trader by thinking positive. You should take at least 10 minutes every day to implement what you have learned in this chapter to be positive.

I trust that you will now take the action you need to change your attitude to being positive and leverage this into being a successful trader. You can achieve anything you want or desire. It is my hope that you will look inside of yourself and commit to being positive and get the freedom that you will gain by ending any habit of being a negative person.

CHAPTER 12 – WORLD CUP ADVISOR

About <u>WorldCupAdvisor.com:</u>

Talented professionals from around the world display their live futures and forex trading accounts in real time on WCA and allow subscribers to follow their activity. You can follow the trading of any WCA lead account automatically in your own account with World Cup AutoTrade service. Program features include:

Transparency:

All trades displayed on WorldCupAdvisor.com are actual trades in funded accounts unless otherwise noted. Details of every round-turn trade made in every available account are shown in the Advisor Performance section; for a free login, complete the "Create Your FREE Guest Login" form on the home page. Profit/loss in the Advisor Performance section is shown exclusive of commissions, fees, transaction and subscription costs; to evaluate the impact of these trading overhead costs, click the Net-Profit Calculator link. Detailed Performance Reports are also available within the Advisor Performance section. Read about each advisor and the specifications of his lead ("Live Update") accounts in the Advisors section. Our lead traders compete with each other to earn customer trust and subscription business.

Clarity:

Subscribers have access to a real-time display of activity in the lead account(s) to which they are subscribed. Displays feature separate screens for orders entered, open positions, closed positions and advisor commentary (please note that some order screens are disabled upon request of the advisor). When you're logged into a Live Update program, an instant message will appear on your screen and a bell will ring any time there is new activity. An email notification also accompanies each new activity, and subscribers can also receive text message notifications if desired at no additional charge.

Flexibility:

Subscriptions are sold on a month-to-month basis, eliminating long-term commitments. With AutoTrade service, subscribers can start a new program or stop an existing one with a single phone call. Subscribers can control their own leverage by adjusting funding levels and adding or reducing exposure to a variety of programs.

Diversification:

The wide variety of WCA accounts gives investors the opportunity to diversify across asset classes, trading products and strategies. Please note, however, that diversification in not necessarily available when trading a single program. Click here to learn more about ways you can diversify your WCA investments. A prospect should evaluate each specific program's specifications to determine whether or not that program is suitable to the individual based on that person's diversification requirements. Monthly subscriptions are sold separately for each program.

Confidence:

We try hard to identify traders we believe are capable of sustaining profitable performance on a net basis over time. Many of our advisors have posted top finishes in the prestigious World Cup Trading Championships®. We also feature accounts traded by noted system developers, authors, commentators and educators. The WCA live trading "incubator" is an active testing ground for new programs. WCA AutoTrade service is designed to deliver same-price fills for leader and followers alike on futures trades; authorized brokers will waive commissions on any WCA leader-follower trade in which a follower's fill price is not equal to or better than the lead trader's fill price (with the exception of trades placed outside a program's AutoTrade block when synchronizing positions for a follower entering a program or liquidating positions for a follower exiting a program).

Risk and suitability:

It is important to remind you that trading futures and forex involves significant risk of loss and is not suitable for everyone. Following any of our lead accounts should be undertaken with risk capital only. Before investing, you should carefully consider your risk tolerance and suitability for this type of investment.

Support:

We're here to answer your questions and provide a personal tour of the site if desired. Contact us by email at info@worldcupadvisor.com or by phone at 1-312-454-5000 or 1-877-456-7111.

CHAPTER 13 - MARKET-ANALYST

The Market-Analyst software is one of the finest technical analysis software packages in the world. It offers many technological innovations and technical indicators that most other charting software packages lack.

It is used by private traders, fund managers and professional analysts from across the globe. In most cases it is the technical analysis platform of their choice since it can do many things other packages simply can't do. It has many popular features and does include many proprietary models developed by many well-known market experts.

The Market-Analyst interface is built using very advanced graphics programing that gives you a fluid interface with powerful alluring data visualization techniques.

It uses both end of the day and real time data. The charts and the analysis all do updates and recalculations with every tick that comes in.

To arrange a FREE trial of Market Analyst 7 please go to:
http://www.mav7.com/lp/tradersworld/?cname=TRADERSWOR

or go here:

http://www.worldcupadvisor.com/craigtrading.html

CHAPTER 14- TRAINING CLASS USING AUDIO-VISUAL DEMONSTRATIONS

You can view audio video presentation classes that explain how to use these trading tools used in this book.

To get access to this class by going to:

http://www.worldcupadvisor.com/craigtrading.html

The class will have 6 lessons.

Lesson 1 – Setting Up and Understanding Market-Analyst

Lesson 2 – Seasonality

Lesson 3 – MACD

Lesson 4 – Stochastics

Lesson 5 – Moving Averages & Stops

Lesson 6 – Fibonacci Retracement & Extensions

CHAPTER 15 - 2015 WORLD CUP TRADING CHAMPIONSHIPS® SPONSORS:

http://www.tradingacademy.com
OTA is the world's most trusted name in financial education for stocks, forex, futures and options.

Apex Investing Institute
http://apexinvesting.com
THE source for how to trade Futures, Forex, CFD's and NADEX Binaries and Spreads

TRADE NAVIGATOR
http://www.tradenavigator.com
The Trade Navigator Trading Platform takes immense quantities of complex data and distills it down to what really matters.

THE BUBBA SHOW
http://thebubbashow.org
Learn the intricacies of options trading from Todd "Bubba" Horwitz, educator, trading coach and author OF "AVERAGE JOE OPTIONS."

WORLDCUPADVISOR.COM
http://www.worldcupadvisor.com
Automatically mirror the trading of futures and forex professionals with World Cup Leader-Follower AutoTrade™ service.

NINJATRADER

http://www.ninjatrader.com

Award-winning software that benefits all levels of traders with trade management advanced charting, market analytics, customizable features and more.

CHAPTER 16- CONCLUSION

Thank you again for downloading this book!

I hope the book was able to help you in your trading.

The next step is up to you. Continue to research these ideas and implement them into your trading.

Finally, if you enjoyed this book, then I would like to ask you for a favor, would you be kind enough to leave a review for this book on Amazon. It'd be greatly appreciated!

Click here to leave a review for this book an Amazon!

Thank you and good luck!

CHAPTER 17- OTHER TRADERS WORLD BOOKS

Guide to Successful Online Trading: Secrets from the Pros

http://www.amazon.com/Guide-Successful-Online-Trading-Secrets-ebook/dp/B00QOBED34

This is one of the finest trading books you'll ever see about trading. The reason is that it comes from a group of expert pro traders with multiple years of experience.

Trading as you know is extremely difficult. It is estimated that 90% of traders lose money in the markets. To help you overcome this statistic, the pro traders in this book give you their ideas on trading with some of the best trading methods ever developed through their long time experience. By reading about these trading methods and implementing them in the markets you will then have a chance to then join the ranks of the 10% of the successful traders.

The traders in this book have through experience the right attitude and employ a combination of technical analysis principles and strategies to be successful. You can develop these also.

Trading is one of the best ways to make money. Apply the trading methods in this book and treat it as a business. The purpose of this book is to help you be successful in trading.

From this book you will get all the strategies, Indicators and trading methods that you need to make big profits in the markets.

This book gives you:

1) Audio/Visual Links to presentations from pro traders

2) The best strategies that the professional traders are using now

3) The broad perspective you need in today's difficult markets

4) The Exact tools that you need to make profitable trading decisions

5) The finest trading education

I wish to express my appreciation to all the writers in this book who made the book possible. They have spent many hours of their time and hard work in writing their section of the book and the putting together their video presentation for the online expo.

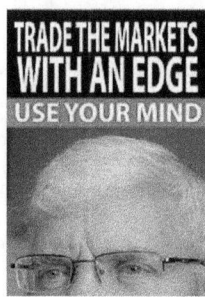

Trade the Markets with an Edge: Use Your Mind

http://www.amazon.com/Trade-Markets-Traders-World-Online-ebook/dp/B00KTQJV50

If you don't have the mind of a top trader, this book might be able to help you develop one. The writers in this book are very experienced and they are here to help you to be successful. Each of them has their own expertise in trading. What you need to do is to read the entire book and find the trader that fits your own trading style and grab it and make it your own. It is just that simple.

Find Success

This book presents to you the best trading strategies of these traders so that you might be able to select those that fit you best and then implement them into your own trading style.

In this book you'll learn:

1) How these expert traders make money and why

2) How to develop your own trading strategy

3) How to improve your trading psychology

4) How to be the trader you always wanted to be. You'll also learn how to avoid the losers and get rid of emotional attachment to trades. To be successful you need to learn to dump the losers quickly and keep the winners for big moves. Another thing this book does it that it gives you the desire to make continuous profits just like the master traders do.

Making profits one after another gives you a fantastic feeling which is tremendous!

Tips for Success
Also in this book you will know who to listen to for ideas from people who have many years of experience and who are seasoned traders.

Crucial Factors
In this book learn about crucial factors in the markets that many experts won't tell you about regarding time, volume and little known indicators. You'll know the right factors that can make you a profitable trader. The unique viewpoints from these many traders can explain why many traders lose and that can help you. The book was designed to help you develop your own trading edge in the markets to put you above others who don't have an edge and just trade by the seat of their pants.

Best Trading Strategies

http://www.amazon.com/Best-Trading-Strategies-Futures-Markets-ebook/dp/B00GG94F78

This is one of the most fascinating books that was ever written about trading because it is written by over thirty expert traders. These traders have many years of experience and they have learned how to turn technical analysis into profits in the markets. This is extremely difficult to do and if you have ever tried to trade the markets with technical analysis you would know what I mean. These writers have some of the best trading strategies they use and have the conviction and the discipline to act assertively and pull the buy or sell trigger regardless of pressures they have against them. They have presented these strategies at the Traders World Online Expo #14 in video presentations and in this book.

What sets these traders apart from other traders? Many think that beating the markets has something to do with discovering and using some secret formula. The traders in this book have the right attitude and many employ a combination of fundamental analysis, technical analysis principles and formulas in their best trading strategies.

Trading is one of the best ways to make a lot of money in the world if one does it right. One needs to find successful trading strategies and implement them in their own trading method. The purpose of this book is to present to you the best trading strategies of these traders so that you might be able to select those that fit you best and then implement them into your own trading.

I wish to express my appreciation to all the writers in this book who made the book possible. They have spent many hours of their time and hard work in writing their section of the book and the putting together their video presentation for the online expo.

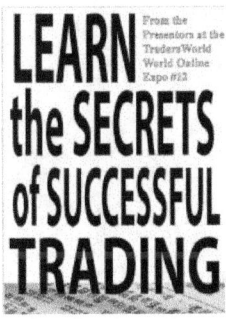

Learn the Secrets of Successful Trading

http://www.amazon.com/Secrets-Successful-Trading-Traders-Online-ebook/dp/B00A2ZIJQ0

Learn specific trading strategies to improve your trading, learn trading ideas and tactics to be more profitable, better optimize your trading system, find the fatal flaws in your trading, understand and use Elliott Wave to strengthen your trading, position using correct sizing to trade more profitable, understand Mercury cycles in trading the S&P, get consistently profitable trade setups, reduce risk and increase profits using volume, detect and trade the hidden market cycles, short term trading by taking the money and running, develop your mind for trading, overcoming Fear in Trading, trade with the smart money following volume, understand and use the Ultimate Oscillator, use high power trading with geometry, get better entries, understand the three legs to trading, use technical analysis with NinjaTrader 7, use a breakout system with cycles for greater returns with less risk, use Turn Signal for better entries and exits, trade with an edge, use options profitably, learn to trade online, map supply and demand on charts, quantify and execute portfolio rotation for auto trading.

Written by Many Expert Traders

The book was written by a large group of 35 expert traders, with high qualifications, most of who trade professionally and/or offer trading services and expensive courses to their clients. Some of them charge thousands of dollars per day for personal trading! These expert traders give generally 45-minute presentations covering the same topics given in this book at the Traders World Online Expo #12. By combining their talents in this book, they introduce a new dimension to finding a profitable trading edge in the market. You can use ideas and techniques of this group of experts to leverage your ability to find an edge to successfully trade. Using a group of experts in this manner to insure your trading success is unprecedented.

 You'll never find a book like this anywhere! This unique trading book will help you uncover the underlying reasons for your lack of consistency in trading and will help you overcome poor habits that cost you money in trading. It will help you to expose the myths of the market one by one teaching you the right way to trade and to understand the realities of risk and to be comfortable with trading with market. The book is priceless!

Parallels to the Traders World Online Expo 12

The articles in this book exactly parallel the video presentations given at the Traders World Online Expo #12. This expo joins these top trading experts together with active traders looking for trading strategies & specific recommendations to help them profit in the markets and is held online at TradersWorldOnlineExpo.com.

From the DVD you'll learn: Time and Price Points; Consistently Profitable Trade Setups; How to Control Fear of Trading; Detecting and Trading Hidden Market Cycles; Position Sizing; Detailed Analysis of the S&P Market, 3 Keys to be a System Trader, Trading with an Edge, Lift off Trading Systems, Monetizing your Trading Expertise; Tracking Smart Money; Trading Price Cycles, Using Options, Mastering Trading with NinjaTrader; Learning Andrews Trading and much more.

Finding Your Trading Method

http://www.amazon.com/Finding-Trading-Method-Traders-Online-ebook/dp/B00DAIOL0E

Finding your trading method is the main problem you need to solve if you want to become a successful trader. You may be asking yourself, can I find my own trading method that will reflect my own personality toward trading? For example, do you have the patience to sit in front of a computer and trade all day? Do you prefer to swing trade from 3-5 days or do you like to hold positions for weeks and even months? Every trader is different. You need to find your own trading method.

Finding out your trading method is extremely important to produce a profitable benchmark that can be replicated in your live account. Perhaps the best way to find a successful trading method is to listen to many expert traders to understand what they have done to be successful. The best way to do that is to listen to the Traders World Online Expos presentations. This book duplicates what these experts have said in their presentations, which explains what they have done to find their own trading method.

If you have a trading method that gives you a predictable profit, then that type of objectivity contributes to your trading edge. The problem with most traders is that being inconsistent will never allow them to have an edge. After you find your trading method that you feel comfortable with, you must have the following:

An overall plan to:

1) Set your rule set and plan and then stick with it in all of your trading.

2) To give you a trading plan for every day.

The trade plan then should:

1) Have an exact entry price

2) Have a stop price

3) Have a way to add positions

4) Tell you where to take profits

5) Have a way to protect your profits

By reviewing all the methods given in this book by the expert traders, it will give, you the preliminary steps that you need to find your footing in finding your own trading method.

Reading this book and by seeing the actual recorded presentations on the Traders World Online Expo site can act as a reference tool for selecting your method of trading, investment strategies and tactics.

It took many of these expert traders in this book 15 – 30 years to finally come up and find the answers to find their trading method to make consistent profit. Finding your trading method could be then much easier when you read this book and incorporate the techniques that best fit your personality and style from these traders. This book will enable you to that fastest way to do that.

So if you want help to find your own trading method to be successful in the markets then buy and read this book.

About The Author

Larry Jacobs has a B.S. and Master's Degree in Business and has been editor of Traders World Magazine since 1988. It's a leading financial magazine which has both classical and modern technical analysis articles as well as reviews of the latest trading books, trading computer hardware and software.

He also has written dozens of articles on how to setup your home trading office and how to get the right trading computer.

He is author of several trading books including Gann Masters, Gann Masters II, Gann Master Charts Unveiled, Patterns and Ellipses and W. D. Gann in Real Time Trading. Gann Masters was so popular it was recently translated in to Italian.

He has reviewed almost every trading software program available and has interviewed and talked to the many of leading traders of the world.

He won the World Cup Championship of Stock Trading® in 2001.

DISCLAIMER

This publication is intended to provide helpful and informative material. It is not intended to give trading recommendations nor is it to replace the advice of a financial advisor. No action should be taken solely on the contents of this book. Always consult your financial advisor on any matters regarding your investing or trading before adopting any suggestions in this book or drawing inferences from it.

The author and publisher specifically disclaim all responsibility for any liability, loss or risk, personal or otherwise, which is incurred as a consequence, directly or indirectly, from the use or application of any contents of this book.

Any and all product names referenced within this book are the trademarks of their respective owners. None of these owners have sponsored, authorized, endorsed, or approved this book.

Always read all information provided by the manufacturers' product labels before using their products. The author and publisher are not responsible for claims made by manufacturers.

Trading futures and forex involves significant risk of loss and is not suitable for everyone. Past performance is not necessarily indicative of future results. There is unlimited risk of loss in selling options. An investor must read, understand and sign a Letter of Direction for WCA programs before investing. There are no guarantees of profit no matter who is managing your money.

Net-profit data under "Leaders to Follow" and "Top Net Performers" includes open trade equity if any as of market close on the date listed, and is calculated using current WCA subscription rates, standardized commission rates (including Exchange fees but not NFA fees) and funding requirements available through any authorized AutoTrade broker. For detail on commission calculations, open the Net-Profit Calculator. Trades displayed on WorldCupAdvisor.com are from proprietary accounts that are either owned by the advisor or are entities of which the advisor is a beneficial owner. Performance data shown for lead accounts is not necessarily indicative of subscriber rate of return and drawdown due to execution, slippage, subscriber funding level and other factors. While great care is taken in the preparation of information presented on WCA, subscribers must rely on their account statements for subscriber-specific performance of any WCA program. WCA accounts do not necessarily represent all the accounts controlled by the advisor. The advisor may have other accounts that may be subject to commission rates different than rates required to follow his or her WCA account with AutoTrade service and may produce results different than his or her WCA account(s). The advisor may have previously displayed other accounts on WCA. Accounts trading in the World Cup Trading Championships (WCC) do not necessarily represent all the WCC accounts controlled by the competitor, may be subject to commission rates different than rates required to follow a WCC account with AutoTrade service, and may produce results different than the results achieved in other WCC accounts of the competitor. To view the trade-by-trade history of all WCA programs in our "Performance" section, fill out the "Performance Reports" form on the WorldCupAdvisor.com home page.

Also please note: That Halliker's, Inc. the publisher of this book is an affiliate of both World Cup Advisor and Market-Analyst.

www.ingramcontent.com/pod-product-compliance
Lightning Source LLC
Chambersburg PA
CBHW070930180526
45168CB00003B/1010